Contents

Enjoy the Book.
Bill Booth JNR.

Liverpool 5

Salt Of The Earth

To be a part of Liverpool 5
You really are very lucky
It is the heart of Liverpool
It vibrates a real warm glow
The people who live and work there
They already know

It has a certain buzz
A place to hang your hat
It has a certain magic
A role not easily found
It echoes through its buildings
To touch the people on the ground

We often think and wonder
Of how it would have been
If Greaty, Scotty and Neddy
Were only just a dream
It places our name in history
Among the real true greats
In Liverpool Five, we are alive
Has history, it dictates

So here's a toast to Liverpool Five
A credit to its name
The meaning of these words
Will never ring the same
Its history is behind us
Its future is looking bleak
It will never be the place it was
When it was at its peak

By W. H. Booth, Jnr

Note From The Author

This is my second book to be published. I have also had a lot of poetry published over the years. My love of writing developed when I was a young boy in the Merchant Navy. There were no mobile phones back in those days!

My hobbies include writing, reading, DIY, football and gardening ... in that order.

I have been married to Cathy since 1970 and celebrated our 50 years together in our house in Spain in September 2015.

We have three daughters: Jane, Susie and Kate. And we have six grandchildren, four girls and two boys. They are Caitlin, Chloe, Evie, and our eldest, Jermain who is 24 who we named our company after 'Jermaine's One'. We also have two very handsome grandsons, one named after my dad and myself, Will, and our other grandson is Rueben. Moth are multi-talented kids and typical boys.

As I hope I have a social conscience, both myself and Cathy remain loyal to our charity work, mostly to do with children. The only person that I would like to meet is Frank Fields, MP for Birkenhead.

What I have tried to achieve in this follow-on book of a trilogy of books, is to illustrate some of the iconic institutions that existed in Liverpool 5 and the part they played in the community.

During our formative years, my brothers, sisters and parents would visit, work and play, socialise and be educated in these iconic establishments.

Liverpool 5 had and still has in its core the very fabric of some of the most amazing architecture. In this city, its churches, hospitals, hostels, schools and community centres, pubs and work places, some still exist but most unfortunately have gone forever.

In this book I try to bring back to life those buildings, the institutions, their functions and purpose, and the part they played in the families growing up and working in this vibrant community of Liverpool 5.

I will base our growing years and our day to day life in many of the above buildings. I can, and I will build a story around them as they come back to life.

W.H. Booth, Jnr

Places Mentioned

Anne Fowlers – Salvation Army Hostel

Collegiate – College

Griddle – Cazneau Street Market

John's Chippy

Building top of Penni

Scotty Road, real stars not celebrities

Jack Browns – Robsart Street next to Orange Lodge Band Room

Maggie Jayne Gordon Street

O'Neil's bike shop

The Barbers

Leo's Ice-Cream Shop

The Griddle-Grain

Burrough Garden Baths

Duffys Chandlers

Homer Picture House

John Bagot Hospital

Paddy's Market

Derby, Jem, Rossi

Lizzie Moss – Bottom of Elias Street

Chris' shop in Conway Street

Taylor Street – Doss House

St Anthony's

St Polycarp's

The Spot

Phrases from Liverpool

Scouse	**English**
Debris Oller	Ground
Ollies	Marbles
Tatter	Ragman
Dixie	Look out
Hey La	Hey lad
Stairy	Steering cart
Messages	Errands

Greaty	Great Homer Street
Neddy	Netherfield Road
The Bagot	John Bagot Hospital
Barra	Handcart
Bunk over	Lift up
Fades	Damaged fruit

Chapter One

Ann Fowler's House – The Story

My first recollection of Ann Fowler's Hostel was as a very young boy. My Nan, who had moved from 40 Gordon Street to a large house in Eastbourne Street, occupied the ground floor. It would be on these visits to my Nan's that we would pass Ann Fowler's.

It was a majestic building. It was enclosed all around by 15ft to 20ft walls. The steps leading up to the house were of a circular shape and once mastered you would encounter these massive wooden and glass doors. As a boy these steps were daunting. We used to run up and down the steps. We got scared as we reached the top step, it always had an air of mystery, quiet and creepy. It had a Victorian presence. It was from another time.

People and places look like that when you are a child. It was a very grand building tucked away at the bottom of a steep brow. The old ladies would sit outside on special days, mostly the 12th of July when the Orange Lodge would pass by for maybe an hour while they laughed and sang and watched delighted, a change from the routine. Some in wheelchairs and taking in the sights on a hot summer's day. If only walls could speak!

Ann Fowler House – The History

Miss Ann Fowler of Liverpool died in January 1913. She had a very long-standing relationship with William Booth who was often her guest. She would have bequeathed a considerable amount of money to him for the use of the Salvation Army in Liverpool. Certain questions however were raised by some of her relatives in July 1914. Mr Justice Astbury decided in the Salvation Army's favour.

The Army's Liverpool benefactor, Miss Fowler, was commemorated by the naming of one of the centres she had recently given to the Army. An eventide home after the owner who had died in the same year she did, 1914.

The home opened in 1928 and was originally called The Grove, but then became the Mary Fowler Trust in 1936. In some reports there is a mention of four centres donated by Miss Fowler, one of which was before the turn of the 20th Century.

Miss Fowler paid for the building of the Edge Hill Rescue Home which opened in 1896 beside the Eventide home that bears her name, and the Ann Fowler Memorial Hostel. We have the best-known gift to her home city of Liverpool, a children's home.

The Army's fourth general, Evangeline Booth, opened her pet project posthumously in 1936, Strawberry Fields. The name had been attached by the previous owner and was to be acclaimed later by four other Liverpudlians. Miss Fowler made all the plans and collected all the money but never lived to see the fruition of her work.

Commissioner Catherine, making a speech at the time, said when she was a little girl she was frightened of this formidable lady, but after she grew up and saw the great amount of work Miss Fowler had done, she was in awe.

Strawberry Fields was bought in 1934 an was opened in 1936 within five minutes of the Mary Fowler Eventide Home, in six acres of grounds. In 1972, four acres were sold for building land to pay for the essential reconstruction. In 1973, the New Strawberry Fields was opened in the grounds of the old one.

Ann Fowler House was opened in 1906 at 2 Netherfield Road. The original home given by Miss Mary Fowler, as she expressly asked that this house be named after her mother, Ann Fowler, as a memorial. It was officially opened by the founder herself in July 1907. It was originally a chapel called the Brownside Welsh Tabernacle in Everton.

To begin with, tickets for beds were distributed by the Miss Fowler Bible Class. Original prices for beds were 4p, 5p and 6p for a cubicle. By 1920 the hostel was so full that plans were made to extend upwards, although this was probably not completed.

It was moved later to Slater Street on 20th July 1983. The official opening on 22nd September 1983. Mary Fowler House was bought for the Army by the Fowler Trust and named after its benefactor by Commissionaire Catherine Bromwell Booth on 23rd May 1928 as the Liverpool Eventide Home.

Ann Fowler House

Research in the delivery as to accommodation and staff establishment. The very first article about Benny's new home for working women tells us that!

The warden, Major Harriet Simmons, with her eight assistant officers, arrived some time ago in July 1907. An article some time later that year has much to say about the hostel's capacity.

By the generosity of our friend, Miss Fowler, (whose help our Liverpool Rescue Officers so much appreciate) this fine building has been purchased for the women's social work of the Army and so offered that it will comfortable and costly accommodation will cope with one hundred and fifty or more women lodges. The General opens a home in September 1907.

The outward appearance of the building is unchanged, save that the first approach, coming up Netherfield Road South, is a big wooden door on which is written 'Women's Entrance'. This leads to a paved yard before a large room, which if necessary will later be used as a bedroom. It is reasonable to assume that this room is being kept spare in case demand exceeds capacity when it could then be converted into an emergency dormitory.

Mention of dormitories bring us to the types of accommodation the new hostel provided, and the same article mentions 4d, 5d and 6d cubicles.

On the floor above (once a chapel) the central space will be occupied by 4d beds and a corridor along the left contains charming little 6d cubicles, a fine lavatory and bathroom. A corner has been built in to provide the warden and her scribe a bedroom. Their offices are inside on the right by the front door. A cosy little writing room for the 6d lodgers is between the warden's rooms and the cubicles are all partitioned. They are of light grained oak, a nice height and beautifully finished.

The floor above has two rows of 6d cubicles along the left side, two large 5d bedrooms holding 28 and 19 comfortably and along the end, which is the front of the building, are three officers' bedrooms. At the front end is a spiral staircase to lead to the gallery and a ceiling at the top of this cuts off at the tower. A new and wider staircase has been built at the end, beginning just where the pulpit once stood.

Responses to Ann Fowler Salvation Home, Netherfield Road

"I remember going pas this building every day from 163/4 on the 46 bus. It was a dark and imposing building. Dickens's Hard Times comes to mind." Dave Hallowell 10/06/2011 at 22.34

"I recall the expression used by older relatives when someone made disparaging remarks about their age, 'I`m not yet ready for Anne Fowler`s'. I always wondered what it was and where it was located. I was in my 20`s when I eventually walked past the building." Rob Ainsworth 14/6/2011 at 20.12

Victorian Fiction Blogshot.com says *"Our society has certainly got its priorities wrong, but it has always been the same. Rich people walking through the city making sure they have their blinkers on. Yes, it is astonishing the amount of money footballers get paid, but I suppose they need to keep their wives in a lifestyle they have become accustomed to with their £8,000 handbags and other designer fashions. The Ann Fowler place certainly does look miserable. There must have been a sad sort of atmosphere in there, it shows in the building."*

"I was a teacher at Salisbury RC Junior Boys School on the other side of the road from the Ann Fowler Home. It was on the corner of Everton Brow and Netherfield Road South. I was at the school for 2 years from 1966 to 1968 and had the most stunning view from my classroom window over the city and cathedrals and Ann Fowlers facing the school." Gina Arymar

"Referring to the comment made by Rob Ainsworth about not being ready for Ann Fowlers – My grandmother used to tell me that her grandfather would warn her that if she wasn't careful she would find herself in Ann Fowlers! I'm guessing she was a bit wild for her time!. Ironically she did end up marrying someone who shared the same surname. I was wondering if anybody has any idea as to who Ann Fowler actually was and how she ended up with a home of this sort named after her? I would appreciate any information at all." Deborah

"As a young Police Officer in 1954 I would walk past Ann Fowler's several times each working day, being stationed at Everton Terrace Police Station (a one-time boys' Institutional School). Although I would occasionally refer people to Ann Fowler's I never had cause to enter there. They ran a very "tight ship!". Norman Morrissey

"When I was a child I was always told that if I kept being naughty then I would go to Ann Fowlers which was not too far from my Nan's house. It was a dark and frightening place on the outside when I was1 6 years old. I am now in my 60s and the thought of that place still makes my spine shiver. Those poor women that ended up in that horrid place. I suppose we are lucky to live without those places. Don't ever let them come back, I'm glad they've gone." H Smith

Pictures of Ann Fowlers

Two of the Salvation Army's most benevolent benefactors were William 'Pickles' Hartley, the proprietor of Hartley's preserves and marmalade, and Thomas Barnardo who founded a string of homes for abandoned children as well as a night refuge for boys and girls.

My name, W. H. Booth, I share with the founder of the Salvation Army General, William Henry Booth. His wife was also called Catherine, as is my wife.

I have to say, without the likes of Mary Fowler, who gave all her time and money to the sick and needy in those bleak Victorian times, that hundreds of wretched souls would have been lost. Both Mary and William Booth created a haven for lonely people to come in out of the cold and share a home and have a purpose in life and a faith if they so wanted. Thank God for the Salvation Army.

Ann Fowler House

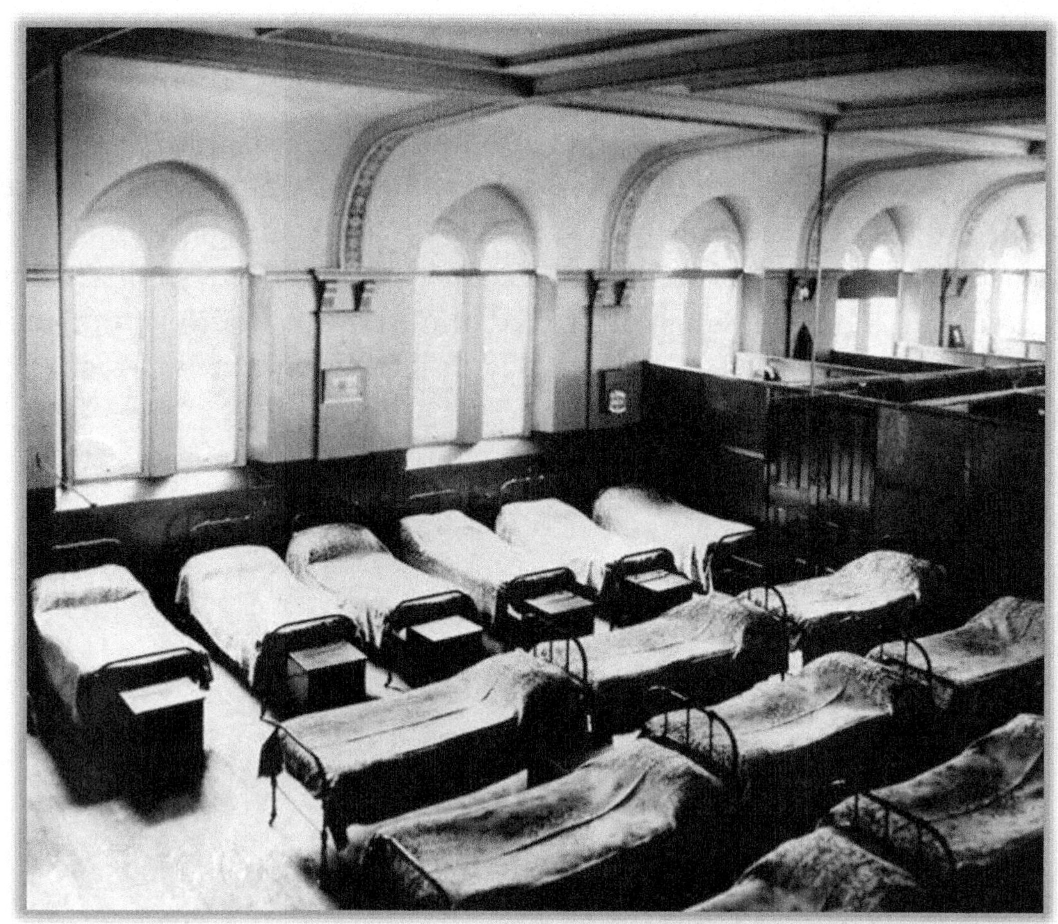

Interior of Home, 1910

Chapter 2

John Bagot Hospital

I have good memories of John Bagot Hospital. Firstly, as a very young boy playing with friends on Gordon Street, off Netherfield Road, on those long summer days of my youth. When butterflies would appear, we would take off our jumpers and leg after the butterflies. Inevitably they would head off towards the John Bagot, across the busy Netherfield Road.

Imagine running up a steep street, and Gordy was steep, then having to climb steps facing St Polycarp's Church at the bottom of Mitford Street, then another steep hill, then to top it all off, as young boys no bigger than 3ft/3ft 6 inches tall, we then had to climb a 7ft/9ft wall that ran down a sloping street in order to climb over and into the hospital grounds to try to avoid staff and patients. Just so we could throw our jumpers over some beautiful butterflies! How cruel were we? Mostly they would die. But we were young, and it was exciting. We would see those butterflies everywhere.

St Polycarp's Church

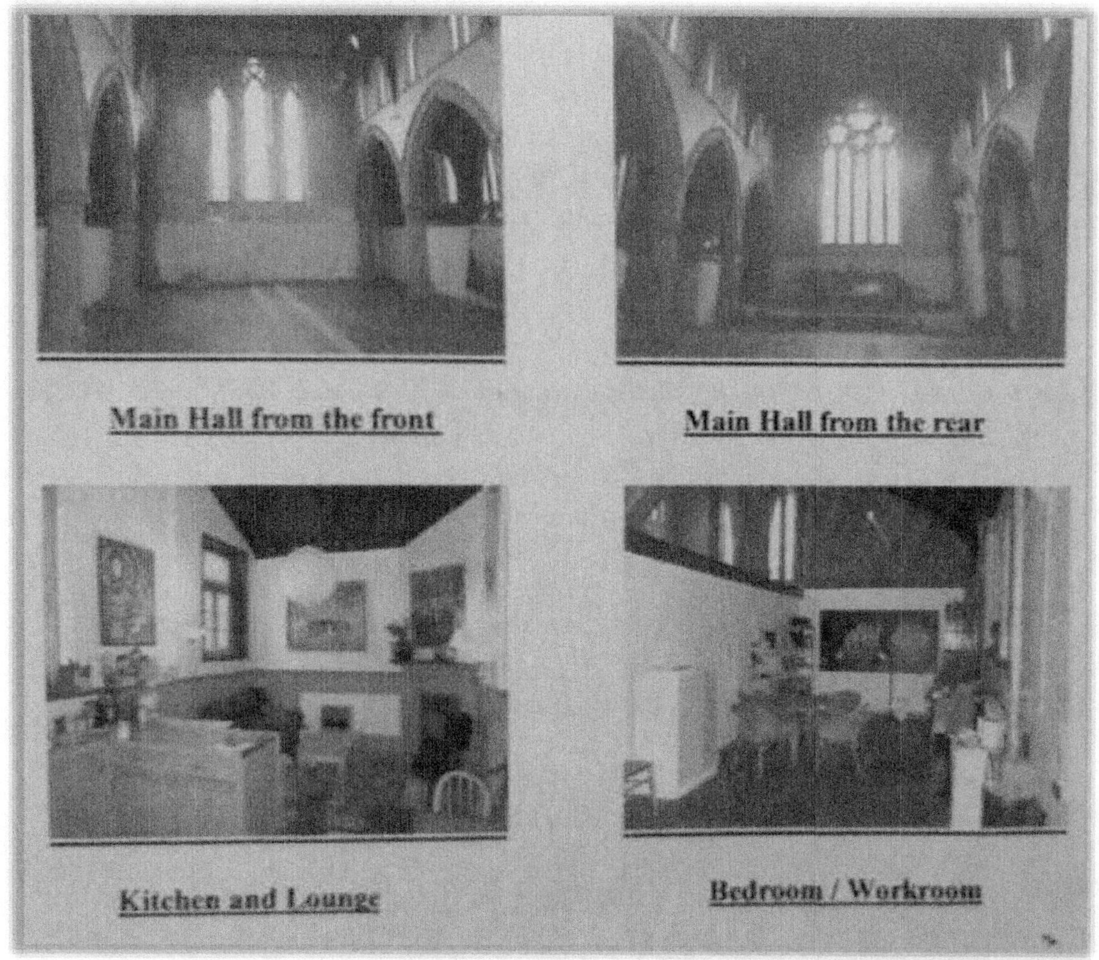

Inside St Polycarp's

In John Bagot it had greenery everywhere. There were trees, grass, flowers, plants, lawns and meadows. We had never seen anything like it. Down Gordy, the grounds and borders and pathways were lush and green, just beautiful to see and as young kids in the sixties we never seen anything like it!

Having climbed into the hospital you were on private land. You could easily hide in the bushes. Sometimes we would climb over about six of us and just lay on the grass and we would take in the view of the city. It was, after all, the best view in Liverpool/Everton and the highest point.

Mind you, our happiest journey was yet to come because we had to dangle from the wall, all 3ft of us, and probably had to drop 8ft onto paving stones. If we missed on the way down we would hit a steel railing that went all the way up to Mitford Street, about 3ft off the ground, which would enable anyone walking up the hill to use the railing as a guide, or crutch, if you like. It was a steep street. No wonder the women had better legs than Ian St John. They were fit! Imagine pushing a pram up those streets with kids in them and two hanging from the sides. The pram alone weighed a tonne. Those women took some beating. All the Everton women were made of girders – a different class.

My other recollection of the John Bagot Hospital was when I worked there. How is that for déjà vu. I was a porter in the Bagot, as it was called in those days. I was working as a conductor on the buses at that time, another of my many jobs I had after I left the Navy. We had not been married long and Cathy was pregnant with our oldest daughter, Jane.

When my cousin, Ted Boland, now deceased, said to my dad, “Does your Billy want a job in the John Bagot?” Well, at that time I was travelling to Walton Depot and doing split shifts. I wouldn’t get home to Garston. I had no car back then, so I stayed local to Walton. It was a bad idea because I started to drink more during the day. How I survived those days, it wasn’t fair on Cathy. We argued about my time out of the house, most days over 15 hours, and my heavy drinking. It went on for years. Like all bad times they eventually come to an end. Later in the book, I got better, to coin a phrase.

Anyway, I applied for the job as a porter as my cousin Teddy was about to give up. I started the job in May 1970. I recall that period very well. Cathy was pregnant and one of my workmates at the Bagot, Tommy Whitty, his wife was due that year. Later that year our daughter Jane was born, and Tommy’s wife also had a girl. So happy days when you think our eldest, Jane, will be 47 as I write this. It’s unbelievable the journey me, Cathy and all our children have been on.

Anyway, back again to John Bagot. It was an interesting job in that no two days were alike. There were six porters working days and one of the six alternatively working nights. Mostly at night was to man the switchboard or now and then were needed to attend the wards to move a body to the mortuary, usually with the help of one of the male nurses. At least one male nurse would work the evenings. Once the priest had left the hospital and the family and had left, and the doctor had certified the death, our job would start. After we had manoeuvred the priest to the main gate after several whiskies, he was local, mostly St Anthony’s. The job had its good and bad points.

As I have already said, in those early days after leaving the Navy, I found it hard to settle to a shore job after being at sea and travelling the world. So, when the opportunity came along to have a drink I usually went over the top as it was on many occasions at the Bagot. As it is today, no health and safety and political correctness, drinking whilst on duty! I would often drink during my lunch break and I would go to the local pub, The Stingo, which was just over the road from the Bagot. I was very much a longer in those days which will come back later in the book.

Back to the pub, I would during my lunch drink maybe three or four drinks, usually bottled Guinness. I knew most of the regulars there and also the barman, Woody, who I worked with at Venmore Contractors when I left school.

The Stingo was only two streets away from where I was born. It was at the top of Robsart Street and lived at Gordon Street. Those days my usual tipple was bottled Guinness and like most drinks, if you drink it regular, you become immune to it. This was the case with me. If I had four bottles it was just like taking the top off the cream of a bottle of milk. I was weaned on Guinness, especially from a bottle. The only person that could drink it as though it was lemonade was an old mate of my dad who lived a few houses up from us in Gordon Street. He worked on the dredgers. His name was Georgie Connor. He was great to us kids. His favourite saying was 'What the hell?!' Noe one could drink Guinness like him!

Though I would have a go after my four bottles of Guinness for my dinner, no food, I went back to work and the other porters had their dinner in the porters' lodge where they would play cards, darts or pool. I was a loner and mostly kept myself to myself. The other porters had been there longer and it was a bit of a clique and I obviously never fitted in. So What! I was happy in my own company.

There were two older porters, Bob and Dave. They helped me a lot when I first started. Bob was funny and a great help. Dave, like me, liked a bet on the gee-gees. We would have a bet together, he'd pick two and I would pick another two horse. It was never a lot, maybe one shilling each. We were never on a good pay. It was before decimalisation, coppers really, it made the day more bearable. Who knows, I think we touched lucky a few times.

Most of the porters' daily routines consisted of the breakfast run in the morning, on the wards taking away breakfast dishes and pans. Then around ten o'clock, we took away on the trolley all the dirty bedding. It stunk as you can imagine. Those nurses had some job. We would go back and forth to the wards all day and if required to lift or take away a body.

The hospital grounds had to be kept clean. The hospital, though old, was kept as clean as possible. The outside grounds were well looked after. No litter at all. At night time we would in turn man the switchboard. The job was very easy and the pay was bad. My only comfort there was the pleasure I got from helping some of the patients. I would always make a rod for my own back. I would go to the shops for the patients, mostly for woodbines. My dad would smoke them. They called the 'the great little cigarette'. I would also go the betting shop and put their bets on. I would visit the wards most days. I took a risk. If I never did it the others would not. I was soft. I still have that social conscience to this day. Most of the patients had dementia. Nothing has changed, it's a killer today just like yesterday. Those days were forty years ago and there is still no cure. But there for the Grace of God go I.

Most of the patients were bed bound so you can imagine the job those nurses had each morning. I have come to know one of the nurses who visit my business in South Liverpool with her daughter, Lil Curry. She is in her 80s and still bright as a button and a great memory. Always smiling when I see her. All the nurses where fantastic. I suppose a lot of the nurses worked there before it became a geriatric hospital. I remember my mother taking one of us when we were kids then it was an ear, nose and throat hospital.

Lil Curry was only in her mid to late 30s then, in 1970. I have a photo of Lil in her uniform and one of her with one of the porters, George Layton. He was one of the porters that had been there a long time and he was still there when I had long gone. He was one porter who stayed within his own circle and as a new starter you would have to perform some initiation ceremony to be part of the clique. I was never one of the sheep and had no reason to come a shepherd.

Lilly Curry *George Layton & Lil Curry*

The initiation would normally consist of some sort of macho game, lifting weights or doing some press-ups. Something that would bring out or show your weakness. Next to them there were one or two young nurses on nights who they would chat up. But I was just married with a son or daughter on the way; you never knew what you were going to get in those days. I suppose the lads I worked with then would be called the Spice Boys today. I kept my distance which I will tell you more of later.

Lil Curry kindly donated the photos for my chapter on John Bagot Hospital. In another photo, we can see Lil with Bill Moneypenny on Ward 4. The nurses in those days were hands on.

Lil Curry with Bill Moneypenny

Bill Moneypenny and Lil Curry

The patients were like family. The nurses got very attached to them. Bill Moneypenny was a local lad, he had newsagents on Netherfield Road and it was from that newsagent that my brother, Alan, had a paper round. He would start very early in the morning and after that he even had the energy to help the milk man do his rounds. The lads, boys, them days will always have more energy mostly because they ate well – no MacDonald's in our day! Just pure homemade meals prepared and cooked by our mams. No stodge, just plenty of vegetables all cooked well. We got to bed early. No television, what was that? No computers, no mobile phones, or handcuffs as I call them.

We went to bed early, got up early, no distractions at all. Plenty of street games, loads of outdoor pursuits, football, cricket and rounders amongst other games. Our Alan enjoyed his time at Moneypenny's especially at Christmas when they looked after him and me mam and don't forget the tips.

Another patient who was on Ward 4 was a man I got to know well both as a boy and a young man growing up around Greaty and Neddy, and as a patient. He was a local hero! A character and if I might say so, the term legend means just that. When people cook for a living, dance, sing and act and drive a bus, that word legend should apply to people who do their job, get paid, and then do their job day after day. They are special and so was this man. He was our local chimney sweep. Today's celebrities imagine them getting soot in their fingernails or hair, maybe it would do their skin a world of good, who knows!

One day, on Ward 4, I was taking the large urns onto the ward when I saw this man. I said to either Lily Curry or Stan's wife, as they both worked together, 'What area is that bloke from?" They told me he was a local man and lived off Greaty. I said, "I know his face". Anyway, weeks went by and I would go off on messages for patients, mostly for woodies. Most people smoked so why not? They never had much. Even my dad smoked woodies.

One pay day while removing a body from the ward I thought I'm going to ask him. Some days are better than others and their memories keep flooding back. They call it Alzheimer's today. It was called something else back in the day. I said, "Can I ask you a question?" He said, "Depends on what it is." I asked him "Where did you live?" He said, "Here now".

We both laughed. He then told me he had lived on Bostock Street. I remembered my dad had been born there.

I asked what job he did and when he had been well. "Guess what? I was a chimney sweep". I knew I'd recognised that face even without the soot. It would have been hard work and long hours with little pay ad then for him to end up in the John Bagot with one of the most soul-destroying illnesses of both yesterday and modern times. How men of his quality, hardworking and independent and proud could end up like that. A virtual prisoner in his own body with no dignity left. It can happen to any one of us. You know what, they could not have been looked after any better at John Bagot. It was a small hospital, people, staff and nurses all had time for each other, they cared. Cared is a mis-used word today. If people are not texting on their mobiles and checking no one has tried to contact them. People look after number one, themselves.

Look around. There is poverty, abuse and neglect. I can say hands on heart John Bagot Hospital had people working there who care. There was about four or five who worked in the kitchen, two cooks and two assistants and Mrs Gallagher who was the union lady. I needed her at one time, but I will come back to that later.

In the engineering department there were four men. Jimmy was one of them. In the boiler house room, two maybe three people, a Mrs Horne was one of them. Then, in the office there were three people. Mr Nicholson comes to mind. He was the main man along with Mrs Ryan who oversaw the kitchen and the domestics and Mrs Fielding was one of them.

Two people were on the switchboard daily, about eight porters in all, as well as the head porter (who you never saw). Brian McCabe, Tommy Whitty and Dave Stoppard were a few of them.

There were probably about twenty nurses on any given shift. No more than fifty people per day kept that hospital open, as well as almost sixty patients. I know it was small by comparison, but it was homely. People knew each other and had time for each other. People could relate, people were interested in people, their fellow man. Why? Because good things come in small parcels. Look at the doctors of today. Would you trust a nurse or a doctor? Not me. Long waiting times, hospitals unclean, patients picking up every bug possible and a total lack of care. Not the way they used to be. They were more personal and smelt better. They are too big, no one knows any one and no one really cares.

Whilst I was working a late shift in Bagot, I think it was over the Christmas period, I was on nights and my turn for the switchboard. There was a skeleton staff on duty and the switchboard was quiet. I went to work with half a bottle of scotch, half bottle of gin and eight bottles of Guinness. During the night the engineer on duty came around for a drink. It happened in those days, we had a game of snooker in the big room. Then we started on the booze. A really bad idea. Everything was going great and thank God no one died. What a blessing. I wasn't needed on the ward after midnight and the switchboard was quiet.

By three o'clock in the morning we were both legless. Me, a seasoned drinker, he was a social drinker and he was paralytic. He fell down the steps and broke his arm and then was off work for eight weeks.

The boiler house wasn't manned that night. His wife was after my guts. I said, when I eventually saw her, I am 21 and Les is 45, what do I know? My cards were marked and I was working, or living if you like, on borrowed time. I had a date with the head porter, not only for insubordination, but also for going over the wall to the Stingo pub numerous times on nights. Someone had it in for me. I was climbing the wall of the Bagot, dropping eight feet into Mittford Street, then going to the Stingo sinking eight bottles of Guinness, finding it difficult to negotiate the wall. I was not a sober ten-year-old in seeking of butterflies with plenty of energy, but a 21-year-old drink fuelled idiot.

The ward staff would be looking for me. Obviously, I had an enemy within those walls and I was in Jankers ready for the sack. I spoke to Edie Gallagher, the union lady, and told her it was a one-off offence and I was well liked and always in work. I later had a petition signed and sent around about my work ethic, but I think as a longer and someone who did their own thing and was not part of the clique, the writing was already on the wall for me. The other porters and head porter had seen to that. I was a threat. I was well liked. Even at a meeting at Walton Hospital and my work and ethos was discussed it was not enough. Mrs Gallagher could do nothing to save me. I was gone.

What I will miss most about the Bagot would be the staff and how close everyone was. I had a great relationship with the patients, the porters in those days and could mix with everyone. People were people and there were no Pontius Pilots. No political correctness, no health and safety, no one over-lording, no Gods. The hospital was well run from the kitchen needle room and boiler house, porters' lodge, and one happy family unit. Everyone had their job and they did it well. They went to work each day and it was well liked. How many hospital jobs say that about today?

The porters even had their own makeshift club under the dining room. The other porters made it up with lights, music and furniture. It was good, and they had a great time. I kept my distance as usual. I preferred it that way. That was not me. I was very lucky to witness in the short time at the John Bagot in the autumn and winter months, snow, sleet and rain, you name it, mostly because we were high up. Jut in front of St George's Church, the highest point in Liverpool and when we had weather, we had weather.

I remember when we were kids in Gordon Street we were right facing the John Bagot. The streets being steep and when it snowed it was great to get on your makeshift sledge or steering cart. When it snowed in the John Bagot grounds it was like a Dickens scene. As it was high up, it was difficult to walk up the hill, or when you left because it was steep and even more difficult for those who had cars. The hospital was very dangerous when you were working, very icy and mostly uphill. The porters soon salted it and most of the visitors that came to see patients were elderly. There were a lot of steps leading up to and down the corridors to the wards and office and reception area. Ward 8 was at the top of a long hilly road.

Aerial view of John Bagot Hospital

*Arial view of the John Bagot Hospital with St George's Church in the background alongside St George's school. Photograph was taken from the tenements at the top of Conway Street by John Bagot Assistant Head Porter, Brian McCabe

The Deputy Head porter, Brian McCabe, took an amazing photograph of the John Bagot from an aerial view. From the 10-15 block of flats in Conway Street facing the Hospital, it shows you how majestic it was. Its architecture was unreal – what a shame it had to close and then be demolished to make way for an eyesore housing estate. I have to say it should have remained and had some money spent on it. It would have made a lovely venue for a are home or mental health facility. It had lovely grounds, the best views in Liverpool and it would have blended in nicely with the present Everton Park which is improving daily. The estate built on the grounds looks ugly and does not fit in and even now, 30 years later, looks neglected, in disrepair and out-dated.

Chapter 3

Cazneau Street Market

This market was in our blood from an early age. Mother would shop there every Saturday for bargains as he had six kids and money was tight. Our mum was a good manager. She had to be because my dad was not always in work. So, she would go to the market for shoes and second-hand clothes. We thought they were practically brand new, especially the clothes, but they were not. We soon found out when someone in school would spot the sole of our shoes or our pumps in the gym and shout all over the place, "Boothie, has your mum been down to Greaty market and bought you some pumps for 1s 3d!". It was embarrassing when you forgot to wipe the chalk off the bottom of the pumps before you went out. Although, you were made up to get them on and get out and play footie.

Most of the kids, if they were honest, would have had second hand shoes and clothes. We would get coats, jumpers, trousers, shorts of all kinds from Greaty Market, or, what my dad would have brought in when he was out 'tatting with the barra', as it was known in those days.

Cazneau Street Market was the place to go in those days. People talked about it all over the world, literally! Don't get it mixed up with paddy's Market. It was a totally different place as I will explain later in the book.

There was only one market on Great Homer Street and that was the end of Greaty and Cazneau Street. It was a place I remember going with my dad as well as my mum on Saturday. It was chokka. There were dozens of stalls with everything you can imagine all laid out in front of you, mostly on the floor. There were meat stalls, you could get any bird you liked: chicken, goose, turkey, capon, pheasant, you name it, it was there. You could get tinned meat, some marked and dented. Broken biscuits, cutlery, glass and china, and furniture. There was a man who sold oilcloth, or lino as it is called today.

Cazneau Street Market – The original Greaty Market

Every Saturday, after the matinee at the Homer Picture House, me, our John, Alan and Rabbi and Chinni, and a few other mates, would head to Greaty Market, which was at the end of Greaty. We would stand by the wagon and then out would come the rolls of oilcloth. They were massive and he had hundreds at the back of his wagon. He would stand there, open up a roll, throw it along the floor and with his stick he would say "Who's gonna start me off at 25 shillings, ok then, 22 shillings. Wait, don't go one pound, come on it's a bargain. I won't have it next week and you'll be sorry."

Later, when it had gone back in the wagon, "OK, 18 shilling, my last offer." Then the hands would go up. He would shout the lad at the back of the wagon, his son I think, "Bring me eight out lad, there's one, there's one and that's eighteen bob love. You've had a bargain today, a bargain. I've been giving it away."

The women would be made up. There would be enough oilcloth for the kitchen, back kitchen and the lobby. The guy who sold the oilcloth each Saturday was loaded and he was always well-dressed. He had loads of gold rings on his fingers and a gold watch. He could have had a warehouse or a shop. Anyway, he was one of the main attractions and would gather more people around than anyone else. There could have been around sixty people. He was the man, he could sell anything. I was watching him. He new his stuff and he was the main man. He must have made hundreds on a Saturday. After he had sold the oilcloth to mostly women, men didn't figure into what was going into the house, the women were in charge. They could live miles away, and that's where we came handy. We would say, "Carry ya oilcloth missus".

Now you would never know how much you would get, or how far away she lived. Big problem, remember were only about 10 or 11. There wasn't many kids overweight. We were all fit and had plenty of energy. But a roll of oilcloth weighed a ton, I mean a ton when you're only 10. So, as you set off you could not go at your pace you had to go at the pace of the woman. That means if you had to go to the end of Greaty your back, and your mates who was carrying the other end of the roll, would be killing you. Remember the woman had to pay the two of us.

They were heavy. You would never carry a full roll and it went on forever. You name the colour or the pattern and he had it. He was there week in and week out. By the time you had arrived at the woman's house your shoulders would be falling off. "Thanks lads", she would say. "'Ere are lads, thanks, a shilling between the two of you. See you next week." Not likely for a shilling. I will remember her face.

We had just walked the full length of Greaty. We were four-foot-tall carrying a ten-foot roll of oilcloth. It weighed half a hundred weight. It took us over an hour by the time the woman stopped a dozen times. If I heard, "Hello girl" or "Hello queen" once, I must have heard it over 50 times. Who cares how much ribs and shanks are. Not us at ten years of age.

T we had just walked half a mile there and half a mile back. For a tanner. That's six old pennies each. If you worked it out in today's money the whole shilling wouldn't even buy you a can of coke. Thanks missus, see you next week. Not bloody likely. We would run a mile if she asked us again. From that day we devised a plan. We would find out where she lived and then give a price. She would then have to make up her mind. She'd either agree or she didn't.

Having said that, if you happen to take the oilcloth, how do you know you are getting paid? That has happened before; all you get is a 'thanks lads'.

The markets had other magnets that you can explore. If you can get up early, I mean really early at 5 o'clock and help the farmers unload the wagons.

Fruit market at Cazneau Street

If we were lucky we'd get a shilling, otherwise you'd go home with a bag of fruit and veg. Me mam was always made up. That was a good day.

At the back of the market was where all the fruit and veg were kept. It was always difficult to get work there. The most we would get was a bag of spuds or some fruit. We would often go under the wagons for cauliflower or cabbage. Once, our John was caught by the market policeman. The police were sent for, for what, faded fruit and veg. Anyway, they called at 40 Gordon Street and my mother was in bed as it was still early. My man went mad because a policeman was at the door. It had never happened before. My dad got up to all kinds. We were no angels, but our poor John got caught. You'd think he'd robbed a bank or something.

My mother was so mad our John's feet never got in the lobby. She caught him on the back of his head and my man never missed. Hey mam, you know what that small incident was the only time a copper ever crossed the door at 40 Gordon Street? Some achievement, five lads, one year apart, one girl (mam laughed more than she cried) the title of my next book, so she said.

Great Homer Street acquired that air of mystique. That famous market, it brought people from all over the world. They would be there every Saturday buying clothes, bric-a-brac, anything from bicycle parts. I have seen them carrying chairs, mirrors, bundles of clothes, shoes. Most of them were Indian and seamen.

On the market, the stall holders would barter with them: one shilling, Johhnny, then it was three shilli, four shilli Johnny. That's what we called him., There was none of this 'you can't say this' and 'you can't say that'. People just got on with it. There are too may moaners today and most of them are men.

Cazneau Street Market was a mixing pot of different cultures, the black, white, the young and the old. It attracted every walk of life and it had a vibrant atmosphere with its pubs, cafes and street life. That mad Great Homer Street and Cazneau Street Market so special. It rubbed off on people of all nationalities, it chiselled them. That's what made up their DNA of people living, visiting and socialising in Liverpool 5.

St Anthony's Church, a refuge on Scottie. Now has the plinth from The Old Drinking Well from outside the Morning Star which was in memory of the famous landlord of the Morning Star (Pat 'Dandy' Byrne). A real legend.

Kids at play. Eldon Place. The good days.

Chapter 4

Shrewsbury Boys Club (The Shrewsy)

The Shrewsy was a vital part of Liverpool 5. It was a meeting place for all the local boys and girls. Somewhere to socialise, to play sports, to listen to music, to dance, and to meet other people. You could have a cup of tea and a snack. You could just chill out and my brother John and I would go there regularly.

Our John was well known there. He'd got with his mate Billy Roberts, nicknamed Rabbi. They were close. They used to play football, boxing and darts. During my time at the Shrewsy, there were a few good footballers who played for the club: Ray Hoyle, Ray Lunt and John Barnwell. They were all good. I liked Ray Hoyle. He was what I call a footballer, a bit like Ray Houghton ex Liverpool. My favourite player was John Marsden, a talent, pure class. Our John and Rabbi were good darts players. Our John went on to become a great darts player. He was left-handed too!

The club was tightly run by Eddie Cartwright and the Rev Roger Sounsbury-Chopper. Eddie was a big man and took no prisoners. You behaved or you were out. He kept a good club and was well respected. He gave a lot of his time to the girls and boys that went regular. There were not that many venues that you could meet up. You know it's been going over 100 years and it's still going today. Although it's relocated to new premises the spirit is still there. It's infection and a real oasis of hope, joy and happiness. It's present run by Mr and Mrs Gorbert.

Shrewsbury Boys Club

The Shrewsbury Boys Club and Mission

Shrewsbury Boys Club circa 1950 (Ken Jones, actor famous in Porridge)

Shrewsbury Football Team, Ray Hoyle John Jones, Ray Lunt and others

Ray Hoyle, John Jones and Bill Booth at the Shrewsbury Reunion.

Chris of Conway Street. His four boys taken at the Shrewsbury Reunion.

Chapter 5

Roscommon Street School (Rossi)

My earliest recollection of Rossie was as an 11-year-old new boy. On arrival I was a very nervous little boy from my last school, Penryn Penny which was a junior school. I was very spoilt there. Having spent six years there as well as the added comfort of having three of my four brothers there too. I felt very safe knowing they were there.

I was never bullied or intimidated. It was a very warm and cosy school and I knew as soon as I walked through those gates at Roscommon, known locally as Rossi. I felt like 'where am I?'. Literally, the playground was full. The kids were playing football and some where fighting, out of view of the teachers. Some of the lads wcrc huge compared to me. I was small fry.

I knew from my first day that I would have to look after myself. No John, no Alan, no Ray. Just me, short arse. Jut twelve months till our john arrived and then I would be ok. But you know, my first year never went that bad. I had my mate from Penni, Billy Baker, and you never messed with Billy. He was massive. Mind you, he cam unstuck when he challenged Tommy Griffiths on the oller in Arkwright Street. No-one messed with Tommy, either. There were two lads of 11/15 years of age. One was Tommy Griffiths, the other was Ronnie Hough. During my life I came across them many times. I meet Tommy in the village where I now live. He still looks hard but we get on great. I have seen Ronnie now and again in Asda, although not for a few years. I was told he moved abroad but he may not have.

I used to see Ronnie as he had a few pubs around Liverpool. He was very active around the clubs. He kept fit well into his fifties and sixties. He was a nice man, a gentleman. He was also a great boxer on the local boxing scene. He fought another lad we both knew who was a quiet man growing up but a great boxer. His name was Pat Dwyer. A lovely man, he had his own gym facing Shaw Street Park. I have bumped into him over the years when he was a cab driver.

Liverpool boxers, who make up the 42 Lancashire Division team for the Territorial Army championships in London on Friday and Saturday, are pictured here during a final training session at the Fraser Street gymnasium. Watching lightweight Private Terry Kinsella (5th Kings Regiment) at work, are six members of the 1st Battalion Liverpool Scottish, who make up the team. They are (left to right): Private W. Davies, Private Derek Thompson, Corporal Frank Evans, Lance Corporal Mick Molyneux, Corporal George Kay and Private Johnny Williamson. Over 100 boxers from all over the United Kingdom will be taking part in these championships, including such well

Back to Rossie. The teachers were great, the curriculum was small, and it was basically sport, sport and more sport. Well almost. The two main teachers who excelled in that area where Mr Bossie and Mr Chisnall. One was small and the other was tall. You never messed with either. They gave up a lot of their time for the boys back then.

Mr Bossie had some great boxers under his wing: Roberts, Peak and Baker. He would give them most of his evenings to train them. He was a great teacher and well respected. You never crossed him. He ended up living close to my business premises in South Liverpool. I would always speak to him and say goodbye sir, a dying breed of teacher.

Then there was Mr Chisnall, or Chisel-Nose as we called him. Not to his face, he was hard. He looked hard. He took the woodwork class and he knew his stuff. He was firm but fair. He was one of my favourite teachers. Well, there were two. Once was Mr Barker. He was off it – a complete mad professor. He could be ruthless when he lost his temper. With that mop of brown hair of his, gone wild a bit like Beethoven, he was a special maths teacher. There was nothing he never knew. If it was hot outside (and the summers were hot in those days) he would be off with the yardsticks in hand, right through the girls' school, and we would march to the small boxed in yard with its 8ft walls all around. He would be smoking a woodbine and reading a paper and we would all be playing football. It was great exercise, whilst measuring the height, width and length of a small exercise yard. He was a master at getting kids to do one thing whilst he did another. He was a great laugh and nice man.

There were numerous occasions when I had to get the cane. There were certain teachers that you tried to steer clear of. They were all hard men, they had to be. There were some hard knocks at that school. I have to say, in pecking order from hard to soft, in giving out the cane, Mr Botham took some beating. That cane was held by a man of considerable strength. It seemed to stay in the air forever before it came down on either your outstretched hand or bottom with precise force. Your hand or bottom would shake for hours. After six of the best you couldn't hold anything in your hand for hours. And that stick was raised it eventually came down at sixty miles an hour and he never missed. Right in the palm of your hand. He was a master of discipline, giving it out where it was needed. He had at least thirty years' experience of it. The others were liberal next to him. For me, getting the stick or any other form of punishment given out whilst I was in school, and I am speaking personally, never in any way caused me hardship or pain. It gave me a totally different outlook on authority and where we were supposed to fit it.

Another teacher that came close to Mr Botham was Mr Williams, or Tony Curtis. He was the girl's favourite. A smart, good looking man, a bit of a playboy. He was a Welsh man and between him and his mate, the younger Mr Watson, they were the pin ups.

I thought Mr Aspinall was a good teacher. He was funny and had a mop of red hair. We always had a laugh in his classroom and he knew it. But if you went too far he would have you. I have, over the years at Rossi, stood outside many a classroom waiting for the stick, mainly for being late. Never for stealing or fighting. I was a coward next to my brothers. I preferred to keep my looks and talk my way out of things. Nothing has changed.

My respect for Roscommon Street has no bounds. It was a school were each and every teacher gave their all and their evening for the pupils in those days. Not every teacher had a car and the wages weren't great, but their care and dedication and effort put into their teaching in every area speaks volumes to Roscommon Street. The school was set out to give disciplined teaching to boys and girls from mostly Liverpool 5.

At least 90% of children at the school would come from poor and humble backgrounds. Some not even able to master a penny or so for sweets each day. It wasn't like today when a child can go to school with £5 in their pocket. The headmaster and all those teachers gave each and every boy and girl and education in every aspect they taught. They had a reunion in the Shrewsbury Club or ex-Rossi pupils. I was asked by Mr Williams, he said:

"Bill I would never have thought in a million years you are where you are today, in a business and employing people, having numerous shops. You were not academically bright. How did this happen?"

My reply to that was:

"To be honest, Mr Williams, Rossi was a tough school. It never gave me a third for knowledge but it did give me a great deal of discipline. I used those principles and guidelines in my life and the way I ran my business. Without that fear of being late, the fear of being absent, the fear of the cane, all these points steer you in one direction and that I one of the reasons I love Rossi. Along with the Vindacatrix Sea Training School which also moulded my life."

They both gave me the confidence to be more sociable. I could mix better. I acquired the belief that 'I could do that'. Having been and come through those two establishments with some credibility and a sense of dignity which I still have today, thanks to Rossi.

Incidentally I can quote my testimonial from Mr Botham, the headmaster:

"William is a quiet, polite boy. He has applied himself steadily. He has been a loyal and effective prefect."

Those few words described me spot on and what I have done in my life. What I have achieved were all due to those days at the Rossi. I try to be polite and treat people with respect and go about my business quietly and steadily and to be an effective husband, father and grandfather

Roscommon Street School

Roscommon Street School

Roscommon Street School

Back Roscommon Street

Looking up Roscommon Street on right hand side Farmer's Ars pub next door ex Rossi cinema. The Bents Pub called The Wyndham.

Chapter 10

Scottie Road

My dad was born off Scottie Road in Bostock Street, affectionately known as Bossi. His dad, my granddad, had a stable where he rented out horses and ponies etc for carting goods around Liverpool. In that street there were a lot of ships trimmers, firemen, donkey men and scalers. My dad's lifelong friend, Billy Wiggy, real surname Wignall, lived in Bossie too, as did his brothers. He had plenty of brothers, about six of them. They were all great to my dad and us lads and Gail growing up.

In later life when he moved to Gordon Street, three of them lived there. The three were Frankie who lived facing Billy and Johnny who lived next door to us. When we eventually left Gordon Street, years later, low and behold, who moved in two doors up – Frankie Wiggy! He as a funny and very nice man. From Luton Grove, Walton, where we eventually moved to, I would often go down to Scottie with my dad. I was verging on drinking age – well, almost.

I used to go in Fitzys at the top of Bossi. All my dad's mates would be there from the dock. They all had nicknames. There was one man, billy, his nickname was Carrots. He would often say 'I'm skint, I haven't got a carrot.' They were all comedians. The pub was full of comedians and singers and they were all big families. Lots of very hard men, you just felt safe knowing your dad knew them. My dad was well known and respected. He worked hard, played harder and could sing like an angel. The pub would go quiet.

One of my dad's mates was Georgie O'Connor. No-one, apart from Paddy Bennett, could drink Guinness like Georgie. He was the king! Billy Wiggsy always wore a blue cardigan in the summer. He was always smart and a nice man. While in the pub my dad's best mate was Tony Bennett. They both worked on the docks. Tony was ships boss. Tony and my dad went back a long way. They were best mates. When Tony died my dad never went down Scottie again. That was how close they were.

Tony was always smart, never in a hurry and nothing fazed him. He was a real mate. As a young man on Scottie, I would always do the bookie run, being young and fit. I would often go to the top of William Moult Street where Dave Higson had a betting shop. His shop was next to the garage and then there was the entry or entrance to where Cilla Black lived above the shops on Scottie.

David Higson was a great footballer. He played for Everton, Liverpool and Tranmere Rovers and he was also a gentleman. He had a mop of hair and he'd have been a great advert for Brylcream.

When I'd put the bet on I would go back to the pub. I would do that all day from Fitzy's and the Europa on the corner of the street. We would then go to the Parrot and have one or two in there. Then we would go to the Holy House. It was always full at the top of Newsham Street. It was called the Holy House because it was near St Anthony's Church. They reckon the Guinness was the best in Liverpool. It was pulled and poured by a true artist. It was always chocker in that pub. You couldn't get in at the weekend. If you swore in there you had to cough up money for the charity box. It was a holy pub and the people down Scottie were religious.

My dad, after a few pints, would start to sing. No-one on Scottie sang like my dad. The pub would go quiet. He had a voice like an angel. It was a man's pub but at weekends the parlour would be full of wives and girlfriends. My mam was not a drinker but now and again she would go down Scottie with my dad for a port and lemon. Another popular with my dad and Tony was the Widdows. Again, the pub was chocker. It was well known in the area and well managed. Every pub on Scottie was very well run. It was close to St Anthony's Church and the people were respectful. Even when the people had to move on, whilst there was a pub on Scottie, they would always come back. They were the salt of the earth the people from Scottie. You would never come across more down to earth, funny, talented and hard yet soft people. Both men and women, the beating heart of Liverpool, its people, its culture, its history. That's it, it was Scotland Road L5.

Chapter 6

The Collegiate College

The Collegiate is a real gem of a building in Liverpool. Grown, it oozes style and class. It was a building I would admire from afar. I knew I wasn't clever enough to attend there, yet I could dream. I'm sure a lot of pupils lucky enough to have been educated there would go on to greater things in their lives. You had to pass the eleven plus or win a scholarship. Some pupils may have been lucky to attend that way. I know a lad, I was a mate of his brother's, his name was Billy Stewart. He went to the Collegiate. He was one of the brightest lads in Gordon Street. He came from a big family and like everyone in those days, not well off, but he achieved it great. He was one of us, a scholarship in Gordon Street.

The Collegiate educated some local talent. Billy Butler who was in a group in the sixties, and he went on to become probably the most prolific DJ on the Mersey scene with knowledge so immense in popular music. I think he will ever be surpassed in Liverpool. He is currently working for BBC Radio Merseyside. He has also worked for Radio City. He has a great knowledge of music and has a down to earth manner and has boundless energy. One of his most popular shows was 'Hold Your Plums' with Wally. He also hosts the Pontins Holiday Camp weekend shows. It was very popular and always sold out.

Chapter 7

Schofield's Lemonade

Schoies, as it was known when I was a young boy, was situated on the right-hand side of Darymple Street, off Scotland Road and Great Homer Street. What an institution it was. When we were kids we lived on Schoies lemmo. We would have it over our ice-cream, as a mixer with my dad's bottles of Guinness and on its own. It consisted of these glorious favours, lemonade, sarsaparilla, dandelion and burdock, and cream soda.

In Liverpool, no-one came near to Schoies. We would often collect the empty bottles and take them back for the money on them. We would skip the wagon on Greaty. The firm employed hundreds and it was a respected brand, especially locally.

There were other brands, namely R Whites, full swing Corona but in Liverpool Schoies were king.

When we went to the shops for our mam we only got a bottle of Schoies lemonade or cream soda. If I could go back I would get a large cold glass of cream soda or sarsaparilla, heaven, and a nice slice of angel cake to follow from White's cake shop at the end of Greaty by the market. Pure heaven, such simple requests, not an iPad, a tablet or a blackberry phone. How cheap to make you happy? About one shilling those days compared to hundreds of pounds today. If you think back, or I think back, lemonade in those days was first a luxury. You mostly only got a bottle or two at the weekends when your dad got paid. No, my mam it was, mostly men that worked those days. If my dad was working we got pocket money, lemonade and ice-cream on Sundays. Such simple pleasures and no selfies!

Schofield's lemonade wagon outside Sayers on Greaty, bottom of Penryhn Street.

Schofields Lemonade known locally as Schoies

Chapter 8

Victoria Settlement

Tucked away at the bottom of another steep street, off Netherfield Road, was an iconic boys and girls institution. It was perched, I mean perched, right on Neddy Road. I say perched because it had a football area with a view to kill for. It was elevated above ground level similar to the Shrewsy. It was boxed in all around by wire, effectively a wire cage.

Its entrance was on the side of the building and the street was steep, like all of them around there. The men and women in and around Greaty and Hayworth Streets, all the way up to Rupert Hill, Everton Brow, Everton Valley had calves and legs like a footballer's. Fit as a fiddle, fitter than the butcher's dog. Only joking.

I know Victoria Settlement, played a lot of football whilst I was working at John Bagot Hospital as a porter, just down the road. I got together some porters, cooks, male nurses and formed a football team that would play them and other institutions in the area. Although I was not a member of the Victoria Settlement I would still frequent there from time to time.

Chapter 9

George Sturlas

One of the biggest shops on Great Homer Street, it sold almost everything in the clothing range. We would get our bedding, sheets, pillows, trousers, jackets, shirts, shoes, haberdashery and all women's clothes too. It was a real store. It was a Blacklers and Owen Owen but smaller and it was on Great Homer Street at the bottom of Gordy where we, as a family, grew up.

There were two floors and a large staircase in the middle of the shop. On the second floor they had household goods, fridges, freezers and washing machines, hoovers, that sort of thing. They must have had at least 30 staff and a dozen or so in the office at the back of the building.

The Sturla delivery vans would often pull up outside our house in Gordon Street where my mother and other neighbours would go inside the van and purchase household goods which would go onto your account book.

The van had a small door that opened and inside was an aisle you could walk along and observe the goods on the shelves. It was basically a catalogue service but unlike today, you could see what you were buying, touch it, and check it before you bought it. Today, you order something online and inevitably it arrives too small, too big, the wrong colour, damaged or even broken, and they call that progress. Women those days had time to look and when they shopped they were thrift and never wasted money on luxuries. Today they will order from a chair, a few clicks on the phone and it is on its way without moving from the chair. There was no obesity or laziness in those days. The women had energy and a chair was something they used to have their dinner on, if they had enough to go around. Most women had big families and I never seen my mam sit down for meals, she usually ate as she worked. Women were a different class in those days. They never knew what the word stop meant.

Sturlas, when we needed string to tie the bundles of firewood together, we would search through the boxes that were either inside Sturlas back entrance or outside. Mostly the were inside. We would always find loads of string which we would split to get six lots out. We never in all our time we had our wood business bought string. Sturlas, also on the other side of the 'Opie' had a warehouse. This was jammed with beds, wardrobes, chairs and couches. It was a massive building, almost like a church. In Gordon Street there was a small door, all kinds must have gone through over the years, especially when it was dark. It was right facing Pakis, a local scrap yard.

George Sturla had a social conscience and he gave a lot of money to worthy charities. He, I believe, was the person who founded the building of Penryhn School. I know that the side door in Gordon Street was the entrance to a night school Mr Sturla paid for unfortunate souls to go and be educated and learn some skills and to have a meal. He was an extremely kind man.

Those names of iconic Liverpool buildings all have a story to tell. Most have gone. Liverpool 5 has been devastated and stripped of all its history. The buildings in time could have evolved, they were built to last, yet they went too quickly. The schools, take St Anthony's, had a lot, even a social club. If the church is still there why not the school? It didn't have to be a school why not something else like a care home, a nursery, a garden centre or a mental health facility, yet other landmarks have gone.

When Sturlas was pulled down it was one of the many household names that died. Greaty, along with Scotty, was the beating heart of Liverpool, not town, not Liverpool1, not the Albert Dock. Greaty, Scotty and Neddy along with Sturlas, Freeman Hardy & Willis, Duffys, Melias, big names like Peagrams, Aughtersons, Quinns, Daglish, Freds, gone forever. George Sturla may be long gone, but his legacy of giving back made him part of Liverpool 5 folklore.

A view looking up Gordon Street with Sturlas and Cobblers at the bottom.

Chapter 10

The Homer

The Homer, to me, was an oasis, a bolt hole from reality into another world of make believe for all kids of my age. It was also a home of a certain Mr Donnelly. Paddy Donnelly, to be precise. He was an institution. He ran that picture house with a heavy hand, you would be lucky to get past him. He knew every trick you might pull. He had seen the lot. He was the commissionaire of commissionaires. He was all lapels and epaulettes, very smart, military and very cunning. But once you got passed him it was great, especially when it was his day off or he was on holiday.

Once inside you then had to wait until no-one walked the aisles, I mean the ice-cream lady or Paddy himself. Then it was your turn to let your mates in by pushing open the emergency doors, then daylight and dozens run in and hide. Then all hell let loose. It happened every weekend and it was great.

It wasn't a palace, more of a bug house, but we loved it and the shows that came on there were the Three Stooges, Abbot & Costello and Roy Rodgers, and Tarzan. You name it we had the lot on at the Homer. If we didn't like the film that was on we made our own entertainment. We would be up on the seats and all the fades would come out, tomatoes, oranges and tangerines. We would have one big street fight and no-one was spared. Before we got barred out, sometimes never to return, that always depended on Paddy, his word meant, and he was the man you know. It was only later as I got older and was told by my dad that his father, my grandfather, was a mate of Paddies. If only granddad was alive when we were growing up, I mean when I was 12-13 we would had got in for nothing! But it was not to be, he died when we were very young, never had a grandad on either side after I was seven or eight, that would have been great.

The Homer picture House bottom of Kew Street.

Chapter 11

Burrough Gardens Baths

The baths at Burrough Gardens were just great if you could swim. But for a non-swimmer like me who hates water, it was a nightmare. Days before we were due to got to the baths I would beg my mother for a note so that I could be excused. It mostly never happened. Either my mother would say no or my dad said no.

I was always wary at my being thrown in by the other boys that could swim. I never liked the smell of the chlorine or the taste. It was an overwhelming place. If I could go in the shower, it had a space at the back where you could hide or sneak up to the balcony and take in the other lads. It was only the boys that went that time; there were no girls there at that time. That would be a totally different story today.

The Baths had a very majestic look. It was great for all the kids living around it from Eldon Place and around Bevs Bush. I would have loved to have been able to swim. I still can't to this day. I have had plenty of chances too, in the villa in Spain or on cruise ships. Cathy tried dozens of times but my heart is not there. Cathy is a great swimmer and so re all the kids. Katie, our youngest daughter, is like me and hates the water.

It's funny really when you think I was in the Merchant Navy. I have travelled the world, be it in the galley, if you like, but never had learnt. I have been out in small boat on the sea going into shore or leaving a port to join the ship anchored, be it on a cruise ship or while in the Merchant Navy, and it doesn't bother me. It's only when I'm in the water when I freeze. As a lad growing up our forte was football, we loved it. I remember it cost nothing except for the ball. We always at Chinni, our mate, or Franny Leonards, and to go to the baths it was the entrance fee and cosies and back and forth. We or our parents never had the money, so it was sink or swim, to coin a phrase.

Chapter 12

League of Welldoers

The League of Welldoers is one of the oldest charities in Liverpool. It served that area of Liverpool, Vauxhall, for over 100 years. Its founder, Mr Lee Jones, was a very good man who started helping the poor people of the area making sure that everyone was fed and no-one went hungry. It has, over the years, carried on that tradition and now does many things to improve people's lives.

As young brothers living in Gordon Street, off Great Homer Street, we would, every Christmas time, take our plate and knife and fork up and over Scottie, over to Lee Jones, as we used to call it in those days. We would get a Christmas dinner and pudding and a present from Father Christmas. Without something like that to look forward to, hundreds of children in that area would have gone hungry. But the League of Welldoers, a beacon of hope, a light at the end of the tunnel. What a God send Mr Jones and all his staff, past and present, have gone on to achieve.

The Lee Jones Centre

Chapter 13

Great Homer Street

For anyone coming from or being born in Liverpool 5 will know Great Homer Street (known locally as Greaty). It was the most important street in Liverpool 5, it was the very heart of Liverpool. Everything happened there, its market was world famous.

Its shops sold everything till late at night and the people that lived there or lived off Greaty were special. They had at their feet the best shopping area in Liverpool. It was without doubt the most vibrant shopping street. It had everything. It had pubs on every street corner. The shops sold all manner of goods, we had famous shops everywhere. You look at there was Sayers, Melia's, Aughterson's, Gordon's, Sturla's, O'Neils, Charles. There were the chip shops, meat shops, delis, ice-cream parlours, paint shops and one of the first off-licences. We had a cinema called the Homer. We had a chandlers like Duffy's world famous. A butchers that was run by two sisters, this was in the late 50s, not even heard of today. We had the best barber shop in Liverpool, start with Jacksons, a lady and gent's cutting hair in a cellar next door to Woollies, the famous Woolworths were else but on Greaty. It was a pool of life.

The seamen came every Saturday to buy clothes from no other than Cilla Black's mam. She had no airs or graces, it was what she did, a local lady doing a great job. The people were rich in knowledge. They had had hard lives. If you were born in Liverpool5 you was a grafter, it was in you like a bar of rock.

There was a variety of shops selling a bit of everything, from Keowans to bicycles. We had the best chippies around. There was Stevensons, the fish was great. Then there was the Greek chippie at the bottom of Aughton Street.

Chapter 14

The Greaty Neddy Football Club

The Greaty Neddy Football Club was probably the best team in L5 back in the day.

The team below is only my best eleven plus subs, having played with or against. Listed in no order, you may beg to differ, this first eleven wold remain unbeaten all season.

1. Kenny Scott, goalie. Simply great.
2. Archie Styles. Truly awesome and eventually played for Everton FC.
3. John Jones. Dependable.
4. Alan Booth, my brother. Just hard.
5. Billy Baker. The draught champ. Very cool and later played for Liverpool Youth team.
6. Alan Young. Dependable.
7. Ray Lunt. Sharp brain.
8. Ray Hoyle. Whelan double.
9. Billy Graham. Genius.
10. John Marsden. The Wizard.
11. Charlie McCaw. Words fail me. Great dribbler.

Subs: Billy Peake, Brian Gaskell, Terry Ralston, Ray Sharkey, Harry Roberts (Henge), Geadie Walton, Ricky Marsden, John Barnwell. Dixie from Kew Street.

Chapter 15

The Inventor Kevin Starkey – Tell Me About It

'Tell me about it', those few words say a lot. I used to knock round with Kevin and Johny Walker for years. I always had a smile on my face, they were unique. They invented The Comedians before them. They were funny. Kevin said those words 'tell me about it' were down to him, he said them words in the early 70s when we worked together for Lester Joinery. We had a ball. They were all one offs. It's not my job tiling, said Sep to ugly man we never stopped laughing.

I remember one day we were in town emptying a bank into a skip. I mean emptying it – there was not a blade of brass or copper to be seen. Everything went into the skip, only to be removed at the end of the day.

One day we were filling the skip with rubbish, Kevin has one end of the barrow, I the other, he was small, I was average size. He had a red beard, if he shaves the beard off he would scare rats. While filling the skip, there was a guy close by laughing. I said to Kev 'who's that?'. He said, 'he could be a time and motion officer'. We laugh.

There was more coming out of the skip and into the back of my mini. The skip was forever half empty. The man turned out to be a Liverpool comedian, Johny Hackett. That's how funny he found us.

I knew Kevin when we were kids. His dad and my dad were mates. His dad and mine were tatters ie ragmen. His whole family were hilarious. I loved his whole family. They were funny.

Chapter 15

John William Walker

No-one followed Johny, they threw away the mould the day Johny drew breath.

He was a complete one off. Funny, unpredictable, had no fear, no pretenders, no words could describe. This guy was unique but maybe I will try.

I would often go to Anfield with Johny. Everyone knew him in the 60s-70s. He would often go to the Albert and all the fans would say, “you running on the pitch today Johny?”

He would say after a few more pints, “put money on it”.

He would mount the kop wall onto the pitch. There was not a copper who could catch him, he would be in front of the kop taking a penalty with his coat, then off to the dugout where Shankly would shake his hand before he was cornered. If he escaped he got a great cheer from the kop. If he was caught he would be escorted out of the ground, only to climb back in again. He was an institution.

One day walking along Cherry Lane, a car stopped and s strong Scottish accent said “Johny”. It was The Shanks.

“Yes Bill,” said Johny.

“Don’t run on the pitch today, Johnny. Please.”

“Okay Bill.”

Did he listen? No, after a few pints he was off. Not even Shankly could change him. The kop loved him and he knew it. Gone are the characters. We’re left with the sheep.

Wherever we went they all knew Johny. He could chew a pint glass down to the rim, eat a pound of cheese and a packet of crackers. Try that without a drink, all party tricks. Not for Johnny, he was a draw, he never paid for a pint.

On day Liverpool were playing Man City and their supporters were on the march up Viena Street trying to get at the Reds supporters. Johny, half drunk, decided to take them all on.

The police on horseback followed him, cornered him, and he managed to get away and ran up the entry. The police on the horses followed him and had him by his goat. Johny managed to wriggle out of it he ran up another entry but with no way out. The police on horseback followed him, Johny kicked the horse in the bollocks. The horse went up in the air and Johny ran to the safety of the Park Hotel where I was. He said, "Get me a pint". I said, "It's your round, I'm skint, try your shoes."

"Honest I am skint," Johnny said. "The copper has got my goat with my wages."

After the match we went to Johny's house. His wife Jean had mental health problems. Before he left for the match I asked Jean to clean my car and I would get her some sweets. I had a blue mini van for collecting scrap metal.

Anyway, I said to her, "Where is my car?" She said, "Outside." There was a mini van, but it was off white in colour. She had washed it alright. In buckets of hot water and bleach. Thanks jean. Car incognito. After that shock she asked Johny for his wages. Johny said the Police have them and she went mad. We went for a pint.

When we returned the Police were there. "John Walker, we presume."

"Yes Officer", said Johny.

"We have a warrant for your arrest."

"What for?" asked Johny.

"Grievous Bodily Harm to a police horse and resisting arrest."

"How did you know I lived here?"

"Your wife came down to the station to get your wage packet from John West Salmon," replied the police officer.

His wages were eighteen pounds. He was up in court on Monday and fined £50. Work that out. I don't think Jean got sweets for a while. A cracker. Timeless.

Chapter 16

Iconic pubs in and around Liverpool 5 – past and present

I am going to start with what I think was the most popular pub and indeed the most famous licensee Liverpool has ever had.

The pub was the Morning Star (nicknamed Bloods). It was the last pub to be demolished in Scotland Place in the late 1960s.

The manager was Dandy Pat Byrne of Irish blood. He was that popular, he had a fountain built in his honour in 1892 facing the Morning Star. He was a celebrity before the word was invented. It is said 3,000 people followed his coffin from St Joseph's Church to the Princess landing stage to be shipped to Dublin to be buried. The Lord Mayor followed in his carriage and all public buildings flew flags at half-masts.

He was buried in Ferns in Ireland and his nickname Dandy Pat came from him wearing eccentric clothes, waistcoats, etc made of sealskin and a top hat in white.

After his death his cousin, Felix Byrne, managed the pub before moving to manage the Vaults.

In Dandy's will, he left money to all the churches and poor houses in the area as well as ex-employees and family were well provided for.

The Byrne Drinking Fountain remained to the late 1970s was then moved to Ponnal Square. Once the area had been demolished it was vandalised and the plinth was found in a council yard. It was restored and is now back on Scotland Road. It rests in the grounds of St Anthony's Church were a ceremony was held in the year 2000. A number of Patrick Byrnes' descendants came over from Ireland and they have indeed built bridges between Liverpool 5 and the community of Scotland Road and Ferns, County Wexford, Ireland.

I personally know of another pub in Liverpool was well known and still talked about, other than Peter Kavanaghs in Liverpool 8, obviously they will never be forgotten and have gone down in Liverpool folklore.

I name below the other pubs that will have been frequented by millions of people, me and my dad included, starting with my favourite and my dad's local.

1. The Newsham, known locally as the Holy House, next but one to St Anthony's Church, you swear at your peril in there or put money in the swear box.
2. The Hal Way House, top of Bossi, nickname Fitzis, run by brother and sister.
3. The Europa, top of Bossi.
4. The Parrot.
5. The Throstles, top of Chappel Gardens.
6. The Eagle, top of Penni.
7. The Foot Hospital, nickname the Footie.
8. The Westmoreland Arms, nicknamed The Honky Tonk.
9. Dunbar Castle of Byrom Place.
10. The Morning Star, off Byrom Place, ex Royal Oak.
11. Birmingham Arms, off Byrom Place.
12. Liver Vaults, of Scotland Place.
13. The Old Cabbage.
14. The Plough, nickname the Widdows.
15. The Grapes, bottom of Penni.
16. The Oporto
17. The Edinburgh
18. The Conway Castle
19. The Myrtle
20. The Brown Cow
21. The Stingo

Bents Pub

10 Questions About Liverpool 5

1. What shop on Greaty could you buy anything from a rubber to a baby elephant, to coin a phrase. Name that shop.

2. Where could you buy the best ice-cream on Greaty? Name that shop.

3. Name the cake shops, one on the left-hand side end of Greaty, and one of the right-hand side, other end at Greaty, one Cazneau Street end, one Darymple Street end.

4. What family had three businesses on Greaty? What were the businesses?

5. Name the commissionaire of the Home Picture House and where did he live?

6. What brother and sister had a shop down Greaty down the cellar? Name the shop.

7. What pub did most under age lads try to get their first pint in? Clue: great wine region.

8. What was the nickname of the famous Echo seller and where did he live?

9. What was George Sturla famous for? It wasn't his shop it was something else.

10. Name the sweet shop on Netherfield Road that had a great little asset. What was it and what did you win?

I will answer these questions in Book 3 when another 10 questions will be asked, to be revealed in Book 4.

Book 3 entitled "The Boothies. She Laughed More Than She Grieved"

Book 4 entitled "Back In The Day"

Body Talk

When your head turns the corner
When you're walking out the door
Then you're not really here at all
When your eyes begin to wonder
As your feet they mount the wall
Then you're not really here at all
When your mouth begins to quiver
As you're walking out the door
Then you're not really here at all
When your body starts to shake
And your feet they leave the floor
Then you're not really here at all

W.H. Booth Jnr

False Hope

In the pits of your heart
Lies a dormant cry
It stays with you forever
On the back of your smile
Its colour locked away
In a place in your brain
Where you cannot hear it
Like the dawn of your smile
It stays forever young

W.H. Booth Jnr

Your Letters

Gordon Street

Dear Scottie Press,

In the March issue of 'Scottie Press' an exiled 'Scottie Reader' living in Bridgewater, referred to happy memories of his childhood in 'GORDON STREET', off Great Homes Street. He also recalled the sadness he experienced when he returned to Liverpool some years later to discover the level of devastation which had taken place in the area. Gordon Street, together with all the other narrow cobbled side streets with their cosy back-to-back houses, had been demolished. I can identify with the feelings of our 'exiled correspondent' because I knew many of the families he grew up with in Gordon Street. Families such as the ASHCROFTS, BARTONS, CRANES, DUNFORDS, GROVES, KINSELLAS, LEONARDS, MACGUINNESSES, RYDERS, WIGNALLS and many others who were allocated accommodation in other areas, many of them having to move to the outskirts of the city. Generations of these families had occupied the same houses in the street for years, but all this was to come to an end in the mid-sixties when the bulldozers moved in to destroy this once close-knit caring community so prevalent in the Great Homes Street and Scotland Road neighbourhoods of yesteryear.

There was a nag-yard at the bottom of the street, Peckenhams, where after school, a steady stream of youngsters could be seen entering the yard with their empty jam jars in exchange for which they would receive money to get them into local cinemas that evening. On the other corner of that street stood Sturlas Outfitters and it was here during the police strike in 1919 that desperate people looted the store taking the entire stock, even removing the carpet from the floor of the store. The street was typical of the streets in this working-class district with many of the male residents earning a living as a dock labourer, seafarer, ship repairer and carter. Most of the females were employed by Tate & Lyle and British American. Women rose very early in the mornings to make their way in all weathers to their work in the market or as ships' cleaners. For many families the times were hard, yet one thing was for certain, the children were always turned out for school spotlessly clean and tidy and not matter where they went, their behaviour was a credit to their parents and teachers. The photographs (1940s) which I have enclosed with this letter, will I hope, evoke some fond memories of this once bustling district where the warm-hearted neighbours made it impossible for anyone to be 'alone' during times of difficulty.

Gordon Street sloped down towards Scotland Road. The conditions were not ideal for football but it was on cobbled streets such as this that many a budding young Dix Dean or Billy Liddell played for hours in 'matches' which finished up with scores like 20-13.

The picture below gives a view of Gordon Street looking towards Netherfield Road with St George's Church towering on the skyline. Peckenham's yard can be seen on the left, and Sturla's on the right. The cobbler's shop on the corner was Mike Reilly's and the sweetshop next door was known as Phil's.

Kind regards,

Terry Cooke

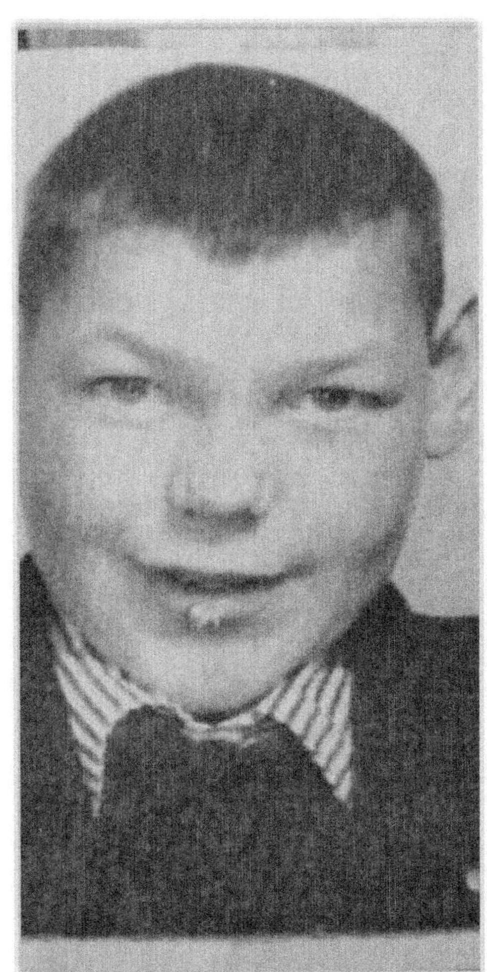

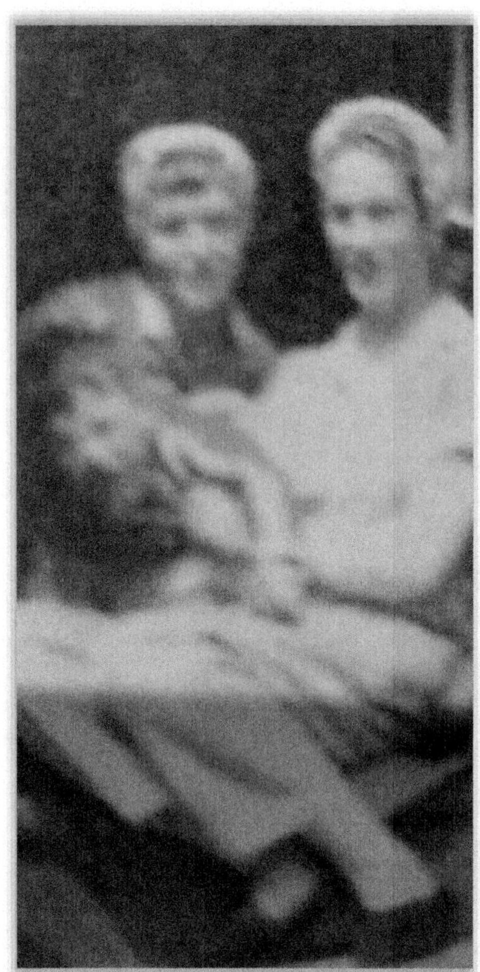

Afterword

The money generated from the sales of Liverpool 5 and Book 3 "The Boothies" will be distributed to the three charities that me, Cathy and all our customers and staff hold close to our hears. They are:

Zoes Place Baby Hospice

KIND Kids In Need & Distress

League of Welldoers

Two new charities we will be supporting are The Carla Lane Animal Sanctuary in Melling and the Shrewsy in Everton.

A thank you to Dougie Mannering for providing some photos. His nan lived in Gordon Street. Also to Lil Curry for providing photos.

Thank you for all your support.

Bill & Cath

Printed in Great Britain
by Amazon

51085243R00044